I Live in a Town

by Gini Holland

Reading consultant: Susan Nations, M.Ed., author/literacy coach/consultant

WEEKLY WR READER®
EARLY LEARNING LIBRARY

Please visit our web site at: www.garethstevens.com
For a free color catalog describing our list of high-quality books,
call 1-800-542-2595 (USA) or 1-800-387-3178 (Canada).

Library of Congress Cataloging-in-Publication Data

Holland, Gini.
    I live in a town / by Gini Holland.
      p. cm. — (Where I Live)
    Summary: A very simple and brief description of what it is like to live in a town.
    Includes bibliographical references and index.
    ISBN-13 978-0-8368-4083-4 (lib. bdg.)
    ISBN-13 978-0-8368-4090-2 (softcover)
    ISBN-10 0-8368-4083-6 (lib. bdg.)
    ISBN-10 0-8368-4090-9 (softcover)
    1. Cities and towns—Juvenile literature.   2. City and town life--Juvenile literature.
(1. Cities and towns.   2. City and town life.)   I. Title.
HT152.H65   2004
307.76—dc22   2003062166

This edition first published in 2004 by
Weekly Reader® Books
An imprint of Gareth Stevens Publishing
1 Reader's Digest Road
Pleasantville, NY   10570-7000   USA

Copyright © 2004 by Gareth Stevens, Inc.

Editor: JoAnn Early Macken
Picture research: Diane Laska-Swanke
Art direction and page layout: Tammy West
Photographer: Gregg Andersen

Printed in the United States of America

3 4 5 6 7 8 9 10 09 08 07

Note to Educators and Parents

Reading is such an exciting adventure for young children! They are beginning to integrate their oral language skills with written language. To encourage children along the path to early literacy, books must be colorful, engaging, and interesting; they should invite the young reader to explore both the print and the pictures.

Where I Live is a new series designed to help children read about everyday life in other places. In each book, young readers will learn interesting facts about different locations from the viewpoints of children who live there.

Each book is specially designed to support the young reader in the reading process. The familiar topics are appealing to young children and invite them to read — and re-read — again and again. The full-color photographs and enhanced text further support the student during the reading process.

In addition to serving as wonderful picture books in schools, libraries, homes, and other places where children learn to love reading, these books are specifically intended to be read within an instructional guided reading group. This small group setting allows beginning readers to work with a fluent adult model as they make meaning from the text. After children develop fluency with the text and content, the book can be read independently. Children and adults alike will find these books supportive, engaging, and fun!

— Susan Nations, M.Ed., author, literacy coach, and consultant in literacy development

I live in a town.

My town is small.

My town is near
a farm.

My town is near the woods.

I know all the people in my town.

I swim in the pool in my town.

I swing on the swings in the park.

My town has
a big parade.

I like to live in a town.

Glossary

farm — a plot of land where people raise animals and grow vegetables for food

parade — a march, usually with costumes and music, often to celebrate a holiday

pool — a tank or body of water where people can swim

woods — a place where many trees grow close together

For More Information

Books

Casely, Judith. *On the Town: A Community Adventure*. New York: Greenwillow Books, 2002.

Geisert, Bonnie and Arthur. *Prairie Town*. Boston: Houghton Mifflin, 1999.

Hubbell, Patricia. *Sidewalk Trip*. New York: HarperFestival, 1999.

Scarry, Richard. *Richard Scarry's Busy, Busy Town*. Racine, Wis.: Western Publishing, 1994.

Web Sites

Scavenger Hunt Scrapbook

www.planning.org/kidsandcommunity/scavenger_hunt/instructions.htm

Create a special book about your town

Index

About the Author

Gini Holland is a writer and an editor. The author of over twenty nonfiction books for children, she was also a long-time educator for Milwaukee Public Schools, both in the elementary classroom and as a staff development instructor for both special education and general education teachers. She lives with her husband in Milwaukee, Wisconsin, and is a devoted fan of their son's two Chicago-based bands.